Mohammed Ali Mankadavu is a writer from North Malabar, settled in the Middle East. His stories in Malayalam largely reflect the agony and nostalgia that the expatriate Keralites are subjected to. Mohammed's first novel, *Munthaya,* was originally published in Malayalam, and it unravels the profound existential crisis and emotional tragedies faced by an unskilled rustic youth on an alien land. His stories realistically unearth the inner turmoil that the migrant workers in the dreary deserts of West Asia face. Simplicity, tenderness, and sympathy are the salient features of his stories.

Email: jiffyali@gmail.com
Facebook: Muhammad Ali Mankadavu
Instagram: muhammad_ali_mankadavu

To the Almighty Allah, to my beloved parents, family, and friends.

Mohammed Ali Mankadavu

MUNTHAYA

AUSTIN MACAULEY PUBLISHERS®
LONDON * CAMBRIDGE * NEW YORK * SHARJAH

Copyright © Mohammed Ali Mankadavu 2024

The right of Mohammed Ali Mankadavu to be identified as author of this work has been asserted by the author in accordance with Federal Law No. (7) of UAE, Year 2002, Concerning Copyrights and Neighboring Rights.

All rights reserved. No part of this publication may be reproduced, stored in a retrieval system, or transmitted in any form or by any means, electronic, mechanical, photocopying, recording, or otherwise, without the prior permission of the publishers.

Any person who commits any unauthorized act in relation to this publication may be liable to legal prosecution and civil claims for damages.

ISBN – 9789948747789 – (Paperback)
ISBN – 9789948747796 – (E-Book)

Application Number: MC-10-01-0931549
Age Classification: E

The age group that matches the content of the books has been classified according to the age classification system issued by the UAE Media Council.

Printer Name: Print Global Ltd
Printer Address: Witchford, England

First Published 2024
AUSTIN MACAULEY PUBLISHERS FZE
Sharjah Publishing City
P.O Box [519201]
Sharjah, UAE
www.austinmacauley.ae
+971 655 95 202

Thanks to my family, who stood up, from the beginning, to accomplish my dream to have a story to be published in English language. I must thank my dear friend, Mr. Ashraf K V from Abu Dhabi, for introducing Mr. Karunakaran Nambiar, the main character in this book.

Mr. Unni Madhavan (Nallezhuth) for guiding me throughout to write this book and his Facebook literary group 'Nallezhuth' admins.

Hearty thanks to Jifshana Mohammed Ali, Mr. Alex Paikada and Sasikala Nair (Pathanamthitta) for their support in preparing the story in English for submitting to the publishers for further work.

Thanks to Mr. Prem Madhusudanan and to the Love Shore group Abu Dhabi.

Thanks to everyone on my publishing team.

Chapter 1
The Discoveries of the Time

WhatsApp is indeed an amazing technological advancement in modern times. Without which it would have been almost impossible for the old faces, who were together three or four decades ago as classmates, colleagues, or mates, to reach out again and share notes after a long span of time. Karunakaran spoke at the tail end of the alumni reunion meeting of the former students of Thalipparamba Seethi Sahib High School, where he graduated in 1970.

'Dear pals, almost all of us have become strangers to each other over the years. So am I to most of you. Perhaps you would remember me when I describe my scarecrow outfit at that time, my cheap baggy-sleeved shirt of worthless fabric which made people look down on me. The lessons used to fly far above my head. I landed up in class 10 just by floating with the flux. In our thatched hut, five stomachs were almost starving. My father earned Rupees three as daily wage, and it was spent on his personal indulgences such as alcohol, beedi, tea, etc. My mother used to get a small bundle of paddy as wages, and it barely sustained us with twice a day meal. For such a wretch, how could studies and homework be relevant?'

It was obvious that this was his maiden performance on stage; his body language betrayed his stage fright. As emotions got the better of him, his words occasionally trailed.

The period of famine during his school days was described as follows:

'After school I would run my way home, about four kilometers away, to throw my dog-eared books to the puny cow dung plastered verandah. The smallest part of the hut was the kitchen, which promised nothing. Still, my stomach would crave a bowl of rice gruel diluted with rice water and spiced with a few garlic flakes and local chilly. My next destination would be the ancient tamarind tree on the farm of Thampan, our neighbor. By pelting a few stones, I would smartly down a few fruits, which I would squeeze into a pail of water and drink to quench my hunger. Then I would squat at a corner of the homestead field, waiting for my mother. She would come in the evening with a small bundle of paddy poised on her left shoulder. It is the sole promise for food of the night and the next day. She would roast it and unhusk it with a thistle before cooking for the cherished supper.'

'Yeshoda would hug her son, pat him consolingly, and ask him to go to the open well to take an evening bath. Later at night, father also would turn up, smoking his beedi. It would be raining heavily by the time the supper is served, and I would relish it with a spoon made of a jackfruit leaf. Another heavy rain would be falling and fading inside me, in my quenched gut,' Karunakaran concluded.

After the meeting, Ashraf, one of his classmates living close to the school, invited us all to his house and even forced Karunakaran to go with him. Karunakaran reluctantly followed us to Ashraf's house.

I furtively asked Ashraf to facilitate another session at home for Karunakaran to speak inside out.

After the customary tea and an exploration of the house, we settled in the reception to listen to the rest of the story. Karunakaran had finished his expatriate life and was practically retired. We urged him to begin where he had left behind at the school.

That November, when the sky was straining to burst into tears, Karunakaran became another puff of cloud ready to break into a shower. He began from his post-school travails.

'Two of my uncles were in foreign country, and the younger one, Sreedharan Nambiar, had great prestige and fame in the village. The elder one, Raghavan, was just another Gulf man. When I heard that Sreedharan Uncle was home, after school I trudged all the way to his house. His favorite schoolteacher, Kannan Master, was there already, talking to him and waiting to receive his gifts from his former student. After a long wait, he met me while I was talking to his mother and enquired about our lives. In the evening, while I was preparing to go home, my uncle pointed to the lungy he was wearing and declared, 'I will give this lungy to you when I am done with it'.'

I looked at the shining foreign lungy, mesmerized.

'Karunakara, take this box to my master's house. You could board a bus home from his house.' Uncle said.

The box was too heavy for me. I carried it across hills, mud roads, and narrow lanes to place it at his house on the road.

'Karunakara, take this; have some food on the way.' Kannan Master offered me two rupees, perhaps as wage, perhaps as he was pleased with the gift he had received. On the way home, I had a glass of tea and sweetmeat from a hotel and bought some jaggery with the rest of the money.

I had scored just 126 marks out of 600 marks in the SSLC examination. Don't be in a hurry to judge that the evaluators were miserly and cruel. I got these 126 marks for free; I had just copied the question paper as such as the answer. When my classmates wracked their brains, scratched their heads, and bit the tip of their pens, I was relaxed and just copied the questions, and 126 was a miracle. I am still amazed by the marks. Nobody on earth is as happy as the one who has nothing to expect.

After that, I was into brute manual labor, including the one at a quarry, often disregarding my tender age and fragile health. Thus, I reached 25 and there was no end of the tunnel. I fancied the prospect of my uncle taking me to the land of sun and sand. The message was conveyed through my grandmother, and he bluntly growled, 'Is he that much ambitious?'

That seemed to be the end of the road. But when Kannan master recommended me, uncle had to budge a little.

****

Chapter 2
A Passage to the Arab Gulf

Sreedharan Uncle was one of the employees at the residence of the minister for health. Wielding his influence, he arranged for a visa for me when he visited India next time on vacation.

Like everybody else, I was also moving abroad with a bushel full of dreams. And I naturally expressed my angst to my uncle.

'Uncle, I know only Malayalam to speak; being so, what kind of job would I get out there?'

'Language is not an issue. I have managed everything. You will love the job. Reach Bombay in a couple of days. The visa papers will come to you through the embassy in Bombay.'

He had let it slip that he was taking his nephew to Muscat as an employee at the government hospital.

'You will be accompanied by one Ashokan, a young man from Kadannappalli village,' Uncle tried to pump confidence in me. As my uncle was known for his stylish life, my perspective passage to the gulf triggered a flutter in the village.

I boarded a bus to Mangalore after touching the feet of my parents and seeking their blessings. Mangalore is the transit point to catch a bus to Bombay. My elder uncle accompanied me. Though the excitement of going to the Gulf was rippling inside, when I boarded the bus to Bombay, the pain of separation from my parents, sisters, friends, and the village environment got the better of me. The image of my poor father, who had a trademark areca sheath hat, dirty and naked feet, a soiled dhoti, a torn-to-rags vest that stank of sweat, and a haggard and melancholy aged face, made me particularly sad. I remembered my mother, who worked the whole day for a small bundle of paddy and came home exhausted to work again deep into the night to feed us. I buried my face into a towel and silently wept. Instead of reveling in the pleasures of the present, people pine for those lost forever.

I was supposed to board the plane to Muscat on the second day of reaching Bombay if my uncle was to be believed. But I had to stay put at Nariman Point for long fourteen days as visa issuance took time. But I had no money to stay that long, and I had no sources to garner that kind of money. My uncle went back home, leaving me and Ashokan in Bombay.

We checked into a shabby, claustrophobic lodge at Nariman Point, run by Mayin Haji from Quilandy. The daily rent was ten rupees. Fortunately, there was a Madrasi hotel nearby. I managed my hunger by having a chapathi and a glass of water twice a day.

I dragged my days away on the generosity of Mayan Haji, who trusted my promise that my uncle would come back with money to pay the bill. Saleem from Vadakara, who was my roommate, also supported me. One day I was terribly hungry in the morning. The white rice I had the previous night had not ever reached beyond my neck. When I gobbled up the chapathi I had ordered, the Malayalee waiter asked whether I needed more. I had only five rupees in my pocket. Still, I fished in my pocket in the hope that the bill might have multiplied overnight. True, currency notes do not breed in the pocket. If they do, why should people like me starve? I had to survive the next four days with the four rupees I got as a balance.

'No,' I emphatically told the waiter.

I drank the water in the glass. I was dying for food. My consternation was writ large on my face. The waiter was moved by the pain on my face. Only the poor understand the poor. I paid for the chapathi and left the hotel.

Bombay is the dream city of many. It was different from other world-class cities in terms of diversity and lifestyle. There are wayside vendors selling samosas and tender coconuts. In the red streets, there were wretched prostitutes with sunken stomachs, dry hair, and painted lips. On the other side, there were affluent call girls. In nightclubs, people get drunk and dance with curvaceous girls.

Ashokan was determined to explore Bombay; he celebrated his freedom. And his visa came early. He offered me the 250 rupees he had left with him. That money was a blessing; I could pacify the impatient and unfriendly Mayin Haji and fill my belly with some food. After a couple of days, uncle came back with the 2500 rupees needed to procure the travel documents. He arranged everything for the journey, and on the day before the flight, he asked me, 'Why don't you give me that 250 rupees, given to you by Ashokan? You have no use of it overseas. And I have no money to go home. I spent all I had on you.'

'Uncle, you know I had no money to survive here all these days. I survived on the charity of Mayin Haji and Saleem. I cleared all the bills using that money.'

I told him truthfully.

'Hmm, then I shall walk all the way home, drinking pipe water.' Uncle flared up and stomped away furiously as if he was going to do that.

The image of an airplane journey I had is from a movie I had watched at Pattuvam movie house, sitting on the floor and looking up, using a one rupee note I had pinched off from the knotted towel of my mother. In that movie, the hero was seen boarding the plane climbing an airstair. But I did not find any airstair. I walked through a door, crossed a corridor, entered another door, and found myself in the cabin of the plane.

The entry into the Boeing plane was similar to that of entering a two-storey building. The cabin had a fragrance, but the fragrance was not as strong as the one I had experienced in Sreedharan Uncle's house. That day I realized that airplanes have a sweet aroma. I looked at the fortunate ones seated on the second floor and settled myself on the ground floor.

The plane taxied on the runway; it was as if a double-storey building was on the move. I plugged my ears with the cotton balls offered by a lovely air hostess, still, the takeoff sound was murderous. My first ever experience of height dizziness happened when I got on top of the tamarind tree on the neighboring farm.

****

Chapter 3
Beginning of a New Life at Muscat

I landed up at Muscat international airport in the morning. I had been asked by my uncle to wait at the post office across the busy road, which was the landmark. The two-way road was bursting at the seams with heavy chocking traffic. Though those machines were driven by human beings, they had no regard for the poor beings waiting on the road to cross over. One after the other they flooded in, offering me no space to cross the road. I stood there like a child on the side of a pool, afraid to take the plunge. I could make even an inch forward. I stood where I was in the furious sun.

The post office building in question was visible. But even after an hour, I could not get there. The sun was maliciously focusing on me. I was sweating profusely. It was going to be 9 o'clock. Still, the sun was blazing. Probably that was the notorious desert sun. I wondered why the uncle's envoy had not turned up yet.

I was thrusting and on the verge of swooning for want of water. The food served on the plane was not palatable, being of an unusual taste. But I had had a glass of water on the plane.

It was thirst, not hunger, that was ravaging me. I longed for a soothing breath of breeze.

A young man with a cap approached me with a smile as I was struggling to cross the road.

'You look like a Malayalee, why do you stand here in the formidable sun? Where are you from?'

He asked me with a sympathetic smile. Somehow I told him that I direly needed some water and that I had just landed up.

Hakim from Malappuram was a driver at the hotel across the road. He took me in his car and drove to the Malayalee hotel where he worked and offered me water aplenty. Then he forced me to have breakfast with him. He was kind enough to contact my uncle's envoy over the phone and conveyed the message.

I had to wait for another hour before my uncle's envoy arrived. Hakim gave me company all along. He was a good Samaritan helping strangers expecting nothing in return.

The envoy, Sivan, drove the car for an hour on a black-toped road, bordered with date palms. We reached a hilly terrain with rocky cliffs.

My eyes blinked upon gazing at the simmering rocks. I had been told that desert was a dry sandy desolation, but I found no sand there. It was rocky soil with dry grass all around. The driver drove the car to a compound on top of a hill. Two towering palm trees stood there like sentinels. I noticed that each hilltop had a house like that.

The compound had multi-chromatic garden plants. There were four houses on the compound, and I was directed to a small room close to the kitchen of the biggest house among them. Sivan left immediately telling me that he had some work to do.

The room was steaming and sultry. Sivan had claimed that it was an a/c room, but I was bathed in sweat. I felt as though the walls were being baked in a furnace. My body was being scalded.

Through the single window in the room, I surveyed the world outside. I could see houses on top of the hills. Upon craning my neck out, I saw a terrifying crater. If I fall into the ravine by mistake, it will be like falling into a granite or laterite quarry.

Shortly I was drenched from top to toe and thirsted for water. My tongue was getting dry. I could see a fair-skinned girl with monolid eyes, and an even face darting in and out of the kitchen carrying food. I waited for her at the door like a Malabar hornbill waiting for the rains. After a few trying minutes, she came my way from the top floor. I gesticulated for water.

I know that kindhearted people easily understand defying the language barrier when one is thirsty or hungry. She fetched a cool plastic bottle. It was a solid block of ice. For me, it was a mystery how they paced the solid ice inside of the bottle. I could not open its cap and reasoned that it was because of my weakness. I was intrigued about how to open it. The girl was not anywhere around to consult.

I impotently looked at the bottle and sat there exhausted. After half an hour I managed to open it. Like a genie out of the bottle, water trickled down. Water quenched my tongue and scalded my throat.

Water frozen in the freezer became yet another item on my list of surprises.

****

Chapter 4
Meeting with My Employer

In the afternoon, the Filipino girl knocked at my door and beckoned me to follow her. She guided me to the main hall of the building.

My employer sat there, a fair-skinned person with a traditional taffeta hat that looked like a conventional measuring jar. His face was gentle.

That tall man of about forty asked me to come closer to him in a booming sound.

'Gum.'

The command reverberated. Looking at my face and pointing his finger, he asked, "oover 'nem?"

The sound reverberated. Trembling and tongue-tied, I stood there, looking at him pleadingly.

He boomed again, looking at me from top to toe.

'Okay go.'

When I stood there, petrified and cringing at the boom, I vaguely heard a lady chastising some people inside.

I returned to my furnace. Then I noticed that a table fan was fixed on the wall in the corner. I switched it on. But the wind was blowing to the wall, bypassing me. Leave alone A/C, the puny fan also was against me. I had seen such a device at my uncle's house but had not operated it; I should have done it.

In my ear, the sounds lingered, 'Gum, 'oover 'nem, go.'

What does oover nem, originated from the big tongue inside his huge cheeks mean? Was it Arabic? Was he perchance asking me my name? but at school, we were taught to ask, 'What is your name?' Perhaps he does not know English. As I know Malayalam only, all other tongues are all the same to me. How could I survive with such a crippling linguistic barrier? I was at a loss.

In the meantime, I realized that there was no Malayalee in the house. I was ravaged like a dejected, banished, and incarcerated being. I cursed myself for embarking upon this misadventure.

I had not yet noticed that my master had begun to call me, 'Ya Munthaya.' I did not respond when he called me so.

The next morning the master ordered, 'Sambati will gum with mathan. Kathitt, puthit in the freezer.'

He left, telling me nothing more.

Words are measured in the house, I thought. I had to toil in a house where words were rationed. It was again like Sumalatha teacher's classroom where she admonished me for scoring nil in the examination.

The master shows off as a big shot, and he does not know English properly. He does not even know to ask, 'What is your name?'

I had assimilated the word gum. I assumed that somebody by the name of Sambati would come with mathan or watermelon.

After half an hour, a pickup van pulled in with a load of fruits, vegetables, and meat. A few Indians darted out of the vehicle to unload the goods. I got closer to one of the Malayalee workers and bluntly asked.

'Are you called by the name Sambati?'

My irreverent question irritated and confused him, especially for calling him Sambati. He expressed his displeasure and asked me, 'Why do you ask me? I am not Sambati, I am Madhu.'

'Actually, my master told me before leaving, Sambati will gum with mathan. Kathitt, puthit in freezer. In fact, I understood nothing. And I don't know how to tell him that I understood nothing. I did not even get a chance to communicate by gestures. So, I asked you.'

He laughed aloud.

'Hello, my dear friend, what is your name? Sampati is not a name; he meant somebody. That is, somebody will come.' Then he pointed to the plastic bag left there and continued, 'Slice the mutton in that bag and stack it up in the freezer. He did not say sampati would bring watermelon.'

He covered his face and laughed again. I joined his laughter like a fool, which I really was.

In the evening, master yelled at me for not preparing the food.

Listening to his yelling, someone from the neighboring house craned his head out and looked. After half an hour, somebody brought a plate of rich and sumptuous food. I also got a packet of food.

I writhed in the hot, steaming room, cursing myself for laughing at Sumalatha teacher whose English class I had looked down upon.

After a few days, the fair girl let me know that by 'ya Munthaya,' the master was alluding to me.

For the first time, I was getting a sobriquet. I enjoyed it with no reservations.

****

Chapter 5
Taking Over the Responsibilities

I had been wondering how to strike up a rapport with the Filipino girl.

We smile at each other whenever we meet. Raising her thumb, she would ask how I was. I would respond with a nod.

One day morning, while handing over the food packet meant for the master, timidly I uttered the strange words, 'What is your name?'

She smiled and replied, 'Name? My name is Rachel.'

Her sound was music to me. It was like being again in Sumalatha's classroom. My vocabulary stock was finished to continue the dialogue.

A few more days came to pass, busy with sundry activities. One day, an old woman in a traditional costume called me to the kitchen. She had a charming face, and her words were compassionate, but I understood exactly nothing as I did not answer. She switched to gestures, lifting her two fingers to her eyes. As I am from the land of Kathakali, I gathered that she had a speck in her eye and wanted me to remove it. Being an old woman, I guessed that I could blow it away from her eyes and dared to move closer. She moved backward and ordered me to stop. She mumbled something and showed me how to use the gas stove and the utensils in the kitchen.

She showed me the cooking methods and recipes for various traditional dishes, one by one, over the days. Imitating Rachel, I also called her mama, which later on I understood meant mother. I found the name very apt.

The master's wife used to shout from inside. Sometimes she used to blast Rachel. One day she came to the kitchen with Mama and met me.

When it was registered on the visa document that I was a cook by profession, I protested to my uncle, 'How could I be a cook, as I had never been one? I have not even washed plates, let alone cook.'

'Don't be bothered. The profession has to be specified in the document as a formality. It does not mean that you have to be one. But let it be forewarned that you must not, for god's sake, claim to be otherwise when asked.'

But I had no means to lodge my complaint, as nobody spoke Malayalam in my midst. Though I had mastered the art of gestures lately, it will not suffice to convey abstract ideas.

When I got engrossed in the job, I came under the direct supervision of my master's wife. With the support of Rachel and the tutelage of Mama, I mastered the cooking that the household had an appetite for. As Rachel called master's wife as Madam, I also did so. Though language stood in the way, the body language of the master, his wife, and children convinced me that they regularly poked fun at me.

Certain experiences make people impotent and helpless. I knew that I was in a fix, and there was no escape from that inferno. My passport was in the custody of my master; it is obviously one among the many Indian passports he has hoarded to blackmail.

Every day, Master, Madam, and children denigrated me with abuse for different reasons. One day, my immediate neighbor asked me in Malayalam.

'Are you a Malayalee? Are you for the first time in the Gulf? I have heard them abusing you excessively.

From him, I understood the meanings of the regular foul words they use on me. I was excited to have a Malayalee close by. His words were revealing. Later, I understood that he was Dr. Yusuf, a doctor at the big hospital in Muscat, where my master was the director. From him, I understood that the place I lived was called Darsait. My uncle was in Muscat.

Three months had passed. I came to know that the other houses on the compound were on rent. I had the freedom only to move within the compound walls. No servant was allowed to venture out of the compound gate. My job was cooking, cleaning, washing, and watering the plants. For breakfast, I was allowed to have a kuboos, a triangular slice of cheese, and a glass of sulaimani.

Mainly, I had to cook a broth of mutton, chicken, and sometimes fish. I mastered that art. Also, I could smartly make mutton biriyani, oven-cooked chicken, etc., and the tempting aroma of the delicious food being cooked would prompt me to taste them. But fear of punishment refrained me from doing so. I may meet with wrathful retribution from Madam, boss, and children. Probably it was my false premonition that the food I ate was being monitored.

The sight of food reminded me of many things. When my parents were engaged in the paddy fields of Narayanan

Namboothiri, we used to get good food. The workers and their children are provided sumptuous lunches.

We used to get a ball of rice, mixed with broken rice and white rice, and mashed-up jackfruit spiced with cumin and fenugreek, added with tamarind curry. It was ambrosia to us, the urchins ravaged by starvation. It was the second-most delicious feast after the Onam feast prepared by my mother.

When we go to Narayanan Namboothiry's place, we should keep a conically folded leaf to receive the food doled out. The supervisors will drop the rice balls from above into the conical leafy containers, followed by the curry served from a coconut shell spoon. Some of the rice balls fall to the floor. I used to pick them up and ate them. Once we are full, like jackals having feasted on chicken, we would play around ebulliently.

It was my habit to correlate my past experiences with new ones. It is interesting that there is no shortage of food here; nay, there is surplus food. But my fate was to starve. Nobody offered me food, and I did not have the audacity to help myself, lest it violated the family mores.

But when I juxtaposed the family with that of the Namboothiri, it catapulted me into a strange state of mind.

One night, ravaged by starvation and heat, I wrathfully pulled at the string hanging from the nasty fan that served none. And immediately it began to swing and console me. When I pulled the string once again, it stopped. Now I got the trick. For the first time, it was serving me and obeying me. That night, I slept well.

For one reason or the other, it was my regular duty to be scolded. It could be for spilling water during irrigation, wrongly stacking the washed plates, or delaying a bit to water the palm trees. The old and young alike ambushed me with abuses.

It was only after six months that I came to know the names of the inmates of the house through Rachel. Mama's name was Khadeeja, my boss was Salim Abdulla, and my madam was Suhra. The daughters were Noora and Abira. Noora was around eight or nine years old, and little Abira was a cute doll with shining eyes and white skin. I realized that she was intellectually retarded. It saddened me. As suggested by Rachel, I began to call my master, Boss.

'Ya Munthaya, jeeb sulaimani nana,' the Boss ordered after his lunch one Friday. I was appalled. I had understood what was sulaimani, its preparation was easy. But nana? Nana is a cinema weekly on sale in the stalls of Kerala, with sizzling cover pages of actresses showing their navels and busts. Does Uncle offer him nana weekly also? Does he read Malayalam? Or has Nana got an Arabic edition? There was no time to brood; he may come down on me heavily if I tarry. I frantically looked for Rachel. If only I could meet her, I could appease him with sulaimani and nana. I was panicking.

I looked for Rachel. I saw her climbing down the steps and consulted her. Instantly, she opened the fridge and pulled out a few ears of green leaves.

When the leaves were mixed in boiling water, the drink looked like basil water. But sulaimani with nana had an enticing flavor. That day I learned that nana means menthol leaves. But even if he had asked me for it in Malayalam, I would have been at a loss because never in my life had I dealt with that leaf.

Thereafter, nana weekly often makes me laugh to myself.

Sreedharan Uncle came dutifully to collect my salary of 40 riyals.

'How is the job?' he asked.

'No problem, Uncle; only I don't have anybody to speak to in Malayalam. The Malayali doctor in the neighboring house seems to have relocated. I speak in Malayalam to stray cats, plants, and trees.'

Uncle laughed wryly.

No matter what, I wanted to make up for the money Uncle claims to have spent on me to bring me here. And one day, of course not at the level of my uncle, but I want to go back home to show off. I would offer a bottle of whisky to my poor father, who cannot escape from drinking. I want to offer a gold necklace to my poor, dear mother, who offered pure love along with the food salted by the sweat on her brow. I needed money to pay off my obligations.

When my uncle left with the fruit of my sweat, I soared high in my flight of fantasy and returned to my small hut, waiting to take on my wings again.

****

Chapter 6
The First Ramzan

As we do in Kerala, I could hear the Muslim call to prayer five times a day from the local mosques.

One night, suddenly, from the blue, when I heard loud 'Allahu Akber' call, I asked about it to Rachel. She tried to explain to me that it heralded the beginning of the Muslim holy month of Ramzan and fasting.

The family had to have their food before the first call for prayer in the early morning but before the sunrise, and the next course will be by the call for prayer in the evening by the sunset. I was aware of the Ramzan fasting from my school years onward.

Thereafter, I had to get up at three in the morning. It was a challenge. I set up the alarm on the old clock Mama had provided me and tried to get a wink of sleep.

Usually, my biological clock was conditioned to get up at five. If I fail to get me up at 3, the consequences will be formidable.

I could not sleep at night.

Until three in the morning, I talked to the fan, remembering Madam who shouts nonstop, the Boss, who succinctly booms at me, and the children, who denigrate me, calling me and flee.

I remembered my poor mother and wept into the blanket, making illegible sounds.

****

Chapter 7
Caught Between
the Devil and the Sea

I managed to deliver the Ramzan month duties perfectly during the first week of the month. In the meantime, I had managed to pick up some Arabic, and I could communicate and understand Arabic a little, thanks to the outbursts of the Boss and the patience of Mama.

I tried to convince myself that Arabic is easier than English to master and that cooking in an Middle Eastern family is much better than working at a quarry in vulnerable conditions. I taught myself that instead of being restive with a banished and incarcerated mindset, it is better to reconcile and get the better of the deal.

I knocked at the door of the Boss's room to wake him up for Suhoor (the food before the first call for the prayer in the early morning) before the predawn call for prayer.

'If you do it to me again, I will commit you to the police. Be warned. Who do you think you are? How did you have the skin to do it? You knocked at my door.'

I was stunned by the tempestuous reaction by Madam.

'He, knocked at my door when my husband is not home. Is he not ashamed? Is he not audacious?'

She pointed her accusing finger at me and told Mama who came by.

Mama looked at me quite surprised.

'Mama, the Boss had asked me to prepare breakfast and knock at the door before the call to prayer. On the day before, they had gotten up late even though I had knocked. Boss had shouted me for not waking him up on time. I did not know that the boss was not home. He did not tell me either. Forgive me, forgive. I will not repeat it.'

I told Mama in my broken Arabic, pointing to the food on the plates.

Madam told something ferociously to Mama and stormed away to the top floor to slam the door.

That day I decided to watch whether the Boss is home and, if so, whether he is with Madam. Even if I missed my sleep, it is better to avoid vicious invectives such as donkey, dog, and shit for nothing. Even in my remotest dreams, I had not fancied such atrocities that she had accused me of.

****

Chapter 8
Treasure

I had finished eighteen months with the Boss and his family. One day Mama called me, and I went near to her with respect. She walked in front.

We reached a shed as large as three or four cow sheds in Kerala. I had never ventured into that part, close to the compound wall. And I have never seen anybody go there.

Mama offered me the key and asked me to open the shed. I began to sneeze nonstop when I opened the dusty room stacked with junk. Mama went back, asking me to clean the shed, dumping the useless things and neatly ranging the useful ones.

Partially damaged sofa set, wooden furniture, children's toys in fairly good shape, and sundry other things I dusted, cleaned, and stacked. Then I removed useless rags.

There were used, Curtains and old dresses. Because of fungi, mildew, and dust, I began to sneeze. I flung out the useless ones. Then I noticed some bags underneath. Some bags contained old papers in Arabic, which appeared to be some documents, also I noticed many files squeezed in. When I opened one of the big bags, I was stunned.

It was full of money! The entire bag was full of currency bills. I was trembling with excitement.

I remembered the fairy tales I had read with friends at school, in which witches gathered treasures and monsters protected them. Mama was the witch, and I was the monster.

I called Mama aloud.

But the sound was not coming out. Again, I tried, this time a feeble sound emanated. I closed the bag and darted out. I rushed to Mama, who was seated on a chair close to the flight of steps to the kitchen, and in broken words and gesticulation, I conveyed the message.

Fee vahid, shanta, okha saiba, kullu riyal.

Mama stared at me.

Then she gestured to shut my mouth. She looked around and found that the coast was clear; she got up and came with me. She was ecstatic upon seeing the money.

If I were a relative of hers, she would have hugged me, I thought.

She asked me to close the bag and take it to her room.

The devil in me tweaked and told me that I should have hoarded it.

But I had no use of it, having never ventured out of the compound. Except for my uncle, nobody coming from outside was known to me. I could imagine the consequence if I shared the news with strangers. In any case, if I appropriate the booty which is not mine, even the small fan in my room will not be able to console me in a disaster.

'Ya Munthaya, today you have unearthed a bag I have long since been looking for. You are good; I like it. You are honest. My husband was a high-ranking officer at the embassy in Kuwait. This is his retirement package. After his death, it was misplaced. Finally, I got it, Alhamdulillah, Allahu Akbar! Five years ago, he was called up by Allah, and he did not mention this money. I thought he had lost it. But I had a presentiment that it was somewhere around. You made it possible. You are a dedicated employee.'

Then she furtively passed a tissue paper to me. I thought she was giving me a used tissue paper to be dumped in the waste bin.

'Go out and eat what you want,' she said.

Before throwing the tissue paper into the waste basket, I opened it. A 50 riyal bill tumbled to the floor. I stashed it under my pillow, and thereafter, every month, she used to offer me a tissue paper in which a 10 riyal note was rolled up in the size of a strange fruit seed. I stashed it under my pillow.

The witch was rewarding the monster for guarding the treasure.

****

Chapter 9
My First Vacation

One and a half years of my life were spread thin on that family compound, with my mind shattered like splintered glass.

I was offered one month's leave per year as per the deal. When I alluded to that to my uncle, he advised me to wait.

I was perniciously missing my parents, sisters, and my sylvan village and when Uncle came to collect my salary, I implore to him.

'Please speak to the Boss and get the vacation sanctioned. I will be back after a month.'

While pushing the money into his pocket, Uncle quipped, 'Let us see.'

It was tantalizing. After a week, Uncle called me over the phone to break the news. My boss had sanctioned my leave of absence. Uncle asked me what I needed to take home as gifts.

I was speechless with happiness.

Still, it blurted out, 'Mother needs a gold chain around her neck, my father needs a woolen blanket, and dress for my sisters and their people.' I came out with a list on the spur of the moment.

I got a one-month long leave, and a Sri Lankan woman was engaged as my substitute through my uncle.

Before going home, Mama offered me a wristwatch. I examined it, and though it looked quite old, I assumed that it was a good one. I had observed the watch worn by my uncle, but it was not of this quality. I respectfully accepted the gift given by my mama.

When my uncle came to collect my salary, I proudly showed him the watch. He examined it and said, 'Do you want to keep this old watch for the sake of Mama? Give me that, and I will give you a new one. When you go home, do not take second-hand things with you.'

I trusted him, being my benefactor. I said to myself that if Mama really fooled me with an old useless watch, it would be painful. I hold her in high regard.

In the meantime, my uncle bought me two watches, costing three riyals. For a moment, I was carried away by a bout of repentance for my ungratefulness and for not trusting my uncle.

After many years, I found the watch given by Mama and worn by Kannan Master. Then I enquired about the price of that watch. It was a Rolex luxury watch used by her high-profile late husband, and it was worth more than one hundred thousand rupees.

'Oh, Uncle,' I involuntarily ground my teeth and growled.

Before leaving, my uncle came to me with a couple of boxes.

'These are the gifts from me; take them home. Let everybody be happy. They expect many things from the expatriates. We cannot let them down.'

Uncle's caring brought tears into my eyes and filled my soul. Though he had collected my entire salary for eighteen months, he returned only 120 riyals to go home.

I had only 70 riyals left after paying for the gifts bought by my uncle; it was the money I had saved from the monthly allowance from Mama.

I did not want to bargain with my caring uncle anyway; he had gifted me with two heavy boxes of gifts. I headed to the airport with two big boxes. Uncle told me that the gold chain for my mother was safe in the box.

Instead of a black string, my poor mother is going to have a gold chain around her neck. It would be a proud moment when I offer her my hard-earned gift to my mother, who had suffered so much to feed me. I was woken up from my daydreaming when the airport official told me that 10 kg of excess luggage was there. The total weight was 52 kg, whereas only 40 kg was allowed. At least the fee for 10 kg must be paid.

I had no choice. It was my first trip home; I cannot let down anybody. The happiness of my dear ones was my happiness. If I failed them, what kind of a Malayalee am I?

I paid the bill and got the boarding pass.

At the Bombay airport, the customs officials were lurking to fleece me. They refused to clear the cargo without bribes. I paid 40 riyals and boarded the bus home with the remaining amount.

I was warmly received at home. Although it was informed in advance, they were surprised when I turned up. My parents were worried that I had lost my job and that the Arab had packed me back home.

'Is there any problem with your job, dear?' my mother asked on behalf of my worried father too. My sisters and their husbands also had come home to pity me.

After having lunch, we opened the boxes. From the first box, a long series of old and soiled sarees rolled out. It disappointed me and my people. We opened the second one. It contained old and useless plates, vessels and forks, and knives used by westerners. I was ashamed and wanted to melt away into the darkness outside. I did not want to face anybody.

It was as if we needed a fork and knife to pick stray grains of rice from the gruel in the bowl, as I was born with a silver spoon!

****

Chapter 10
On My Own

My mother was not able to repay the money she had borrowed from Kannan Master for the marriage of my sister, Parvathy.

Mother had borrowed ten thousand rupees, and Uncle had volunteered to repay it on Mother's behalf. Two years had passed, and he had not honored his commitment.

Two weeks after joining duty back at Darsait, my mother sent a letter asking me to remind my uncle about this. As I had no money to show off as a Gulf man in my village, I pawned Karthika's jewelry and entertained my friends.

I freaked out with my friends, picnicking and offering liquor. Every man back from the Gulf is supposed to do so. Even if you are a pauper, you cannot show it. I also had to do it with borrowed money.

As my uncle claims my salary every month as a right, I decided to confront him with my mother's letter. I wondered why my salary was not given to me, and that too after sweating my blood.

Though my uncle had arranged this job, I thought that it was high time to be on my own. Uncle sat on my cot, asking me about my visit to my home country.

I brazenly brought up the issue of my mother's letter to my uncle, who believes that my salary was his right. He said that the committed amount could be cleared in three installments. Then I blew up my top.

'No chance, clear it in one go, which is the gentleman's route,' I said.

Uncle was taken aback by the transformation in this servile me.

Then I opened up Pandora's box of pent-up frustrations. I was piqued that even after claiming my entire salary, I was not able to go home with a suitable gift for my mother. I let him know that I was not an idiot and could read between the lines.

'Now you have become too big for me, hereinafter you may manage your salary. In the beginning, I collected your salary to make up for the money I spent on you. Then I thought that it was safe to keep your money with me. For safe keeping, I took it.'

Uncle was telling me so to cool me down. And he did not mean it.

But I emphatically said, 'Sorry Uncle, hereinafter I will manage my salary.'

****

Chapter 11
Suicide

Every day, one of the helping hands at my boss's office used to bring daily needed consumables home. At that time, while opening the gates for them or when closing the gates, I used to see Balakrishnan occasionally, a helper in the house across the road.

I never took the initiative to get an opportunity to go and meet him. It was my uncle who had arranged a visa for him also. As he did not have a good name in my village, I used to steer clear of him. Now, even in in this country, I had no enthusiasm to keep in touch with him, even though he was close by.

While opening the gate, often I could see him engrossed in one job or the other, such as washing the car, watering the plants, etc. While opening or closing the gate, by way of greeting, I would raise my hand to him. But on a certain day, I happened to exchange a few words with him. Among other things, I told him that everybody in the family used to call me Munthaya.

'Karaunakara, it is the most derogatory word in Arabic. Its meaning is very obnoxious. Your condition is indeed very sad.'

Balakrishnan made me deeply distressed.

I was worked up; I said goodbye to Balakrishnan in a hurry, closed the gate, and stormed back, and my blood was boiling.

In the meantime, Rachel had left her job and gone back home. After her, many other maids came from Sri Lanka or the Philippines. But nobody stayed on the job for long. As Madam was a vicious tyrant, nobody could tolerate her. As I did not have the contacts or expertise for a better job, I had no choice. I believed that I had gotten the best job, given my poor accomplishments.

With the recommendation of an Indian friend of the Boss, a fifty-year-old Goan lady called Imelda joined the family as a maid. She had many years of experience in the area.

She was a slow and lethargic lady; she was very slow in doing things. Hence, Madam used to blast her very often and I had seen her weeping and talking to herself in solitude.

Whenever we met, she would reluctantly smile and would avoid the company. I suspected that she was under serious mental tension.

'Munthaya, ya Munthaya.'

It was a night when the Boss was not at home. Madam was panic-stricken. I rushed to the top floor.

She was waiting for me and gestured to follow her to the window. She looked out through the window and said, 'Ya Munthaya, look there; Imelda is lying there. How did she get there? Go and check what happened. I am disturbed; what are all these happening?'

Madam was trembling.

When I looked out in the evening light, I noticed that Imelda was still alive. As I was aware of the law of the land,

I thought it would be better not to dart to the site alone. I telephoned Balakrishnan. I wanted to have a witnessing case something untoward happened to Imelda. When we got there, she was in the terminal stage.

Madam called the police and also an ambulance. The police took me and Madam to the police station.

The police informed us that Imelda was no more.

'Ya rayyal, your egg, your egg?'

A senior police officer asked. I did not understand.

I was the one who had served her food that night. It had a boiled egg also. I guessed that the egg had killed her. I was frightened. My heart was pounding aloud. I trembled at the prospect of being imprisoned for the rest of my life.

A young police officer, observing the interrogation, explained to me what was meant by your egg. He was asking what my age was. I laughed to myself.

He asked me many more questions.

'Did you push her to death? Did Madam push her to death? Or did you both do it? You know everything, out with the truth, how did she land there?'

The interrogation dragged on.

Simultaneously, Madam was also being interrogated in another room. At last, we were released. On the way back Madam asked, 'Did the police ask you about me?'

'Yes, Madam, I told them that you both were on good terms. And that you both had parted amicably last night'

'Yes, very good, Munthaya.' She got into the car quite pleased.

The next day, Uncle called me over the phone.

'I heard that you are behind the murder. Balakrishnan told me that you had an illicit relationship with her and that the note she had left behind says that you had molested her.'

My eyes welled up; I had no words to tell him.

****

Chapter 12
Munthaya

Four years came to pass, with my days filled with the Munthaya and other choice invectives. In the meantime, I had visited Kerala three times. As my salary was managed by me, I could take my own decisions. I had come into contact with many home going Malayalees. and through them, I had established a network of connections in the area nearby the boss's house.

I went home for the next vacation.

Under my mother's influence, I married Vasanthy. She was a loving wife, and the limited number of days, saturated with love, burned out very fast. When I was ready to leave, Vasanthy fell at my feet, urging me not to go.

'Dear, don't leave me alone; we can make a living here; I cannot suffer this separation; stay back, please.'

She was not leaving my feet.

I was in a fix; separation was heart-wrenching.

Her point of view also was correct. I was leaving her behind to live in a small house of strangers. In my absence, she will be lonely and isolated. Still, I had no other go. In fact, I had not even contemplated a different option.

I was translating my teenage dreams and aspirations to reality by pooling up my salary and borrowing to meet the demands. I never failed to entertain my friends. At that time, the Gulf Malayalees were competing to show off in the villages. When the wretched get some money, they celebrate their freedom as if there was no tomorrow. I was not an exception. Hence, I had many financial liabilities, and I was not in a position to heed Vasanthi's entreaties.

I left her behind with a bleeding soul.

I was eventually returning to the familiar domestic environment of my boss.

I was already experiencing the spring and summer of my life. Changes were happening to me slowly and silently. I was becoming ill-tempered. I think I could not concentrate on my duties. Vasanthi's tears were influencing me to be resolute.

My mind was traveling fast. Crossing the sea. Our mind can circumnavigate the globe many times in a fraction of a second, amazing indeed.

Before the Boss boarded his car, I had to wash it sparkling clean. If he noticed a single blemish, I had it. When he was gone, I had to attend to the duties on the compound. I would converse with plants and flowers. I would fluff the flowers softly and lovingly. I would tell my sorrows to the palm trees. They only were the silent witnesses to the atrocities I suffer.

It seemed futile to pull on with the tyrants. I thought of leaving the job, despite the love of Mama. But I had to clear the loans as I had squandered beyond my means while at home. Also, I still had to offer a gold chain to my mother.

The next day was Friday, a holiday when the Boss is at home. Hence, my day will be very busy. A new load of household items had arrived to add to the luxurious look of the interior. The items looked like painted pottery. It made me remember the Keshavan and Yesoda potter couple, who used to come to our village as pottery peddlers.

Some of the pots were as large as barrels. They had garish and attractive paintings. The Boss supervised my work and followed me, giving furious commands.

When I placed the barrel at the corner of a room as commanded, it made a sound, and the Boss shouted, 'Ya Munthaya, Munthaya.'

The obscene word reminded me of what Balakrishnan had told me. My blood boiled, and muscles on my face tensed.

Had there been a mirror on the wall, I could have seen my red face. If I had seen my face, nobody knows how I would have reacted.

'Munthaya, not there; place it here. Idiot you are. Eat, snore and get fat; nothing else you do.'

Madam would shout at me when I obeyed the orders from the Boss. It was Madam's style to blast me and make me work like a slave.

By midday, Madam, who was at an advanced stage of pregnancy, went to the hospital, for a checkup.

'Munthaya, this clock costs a fortune. If it is damaged while you install it on the wall, Munthaya, I will break your head.'

Again Munthaya.

Balakrishnan had told me that it was a derogatory word. I realized that the Boss and his madam are becoming more and more pugnacious. I stood on a chair and hammered in a nail on the wall to fix the clock. When I again got on the chair with the clock, the Boss threatened again.

Then my sorrows turned into rage. I stared at him from the chair. I got down from the chair and went to him.

I laid the clock on a sofa safely. Then in a bout of murderous hysteria, I shouted, 'Then let it be so; break my head first. Kill me, please. I have suffered enough. You say I am an idiot, a donkey, a cur, a useless, and again that I am a Munthaya. Then dismiss me. No need to feed this donkey for nothing; I don't need this job, and I want to go forthwith. I must go now. You had been foul-mouthing me for years. And you call me a Munthaya time and again. I am done with you. I had been so loyal, and even your children call me a donkey and tell me that I am here only to eat.'

With my broken Arabic and gestures, I conveyed the message, and the Boss understood my state of mind.

'Even fangless snakes sting you when their life is threatened,' we have heard this adage.

I had never heard that attack is the best form of defense, but practically, I had done something to that effect. On looking back, my reaction served that purpose.

My boss was stunned by my outburst. Mama came into the hall from inside hearing me shout.

The children huddled up to watch the spectacle; they stopped running about. Everybody was taken aback. They were all surprised by my fury.

I suspended all work and retired to my room. I had dived into a book I had brought from home, books have the capacity to cool down troubled minds, I realized.

Madam returned by five in the evening. As a formality, I went to her and said that I was leaving.

'Where to?'

'I have got a better job, and I am switching over.'

'What is your issue here?'

I explained what had transpired in her absence. She listened to me keenly.

'So that is why you are leaving?' she asked at last.

'Not only that but I also got a better salary package.'

'How much will you get there?

'80 riyals,' I blurted out impulsively.

'How much do you get here?'

'60 riyals.'

'Then I will give you 20 more; it is between us; don't tell anybody. So, you will get 80 riyals. Don't go anywhere; stay, please.'

I was surprised that she was polite and talking to me with some respect.

It is still a mystery what invisible forces emboldened me to talk to Madam and secure a salary hike.

Probably after discussing this with Madam, the Boss called me in the evening.

'Munthaya, go and bring your passport copy,' he said calmly and affectionately.

I guessed that he was going to give me the marching orders; from his body language, it was obvious that he was done with me.

I had blurted out many absurdities in a bout of madness; frustration had gotten the better of me. If he packs me off, I have no source of income. And I had been showing off in the village. Again, I will have to slog in the quarries. The village will look down on me. These thoughts streaked through me when I collected the copy of my passport from a bag kept in the kitchen. I produced the document before the Boss, but I did not have the humility to ask the Boss not to dismiss me.

Boss examined the passport copy and affectionately asked me to read the name written on it.

'Look, what is your name?'

'Mundayattu Veettil Ratnakaran,' I read.

'Yes, Munthayat house Ratna,' Boss aped me.

'That is why we call you Munthaya. Hereinafter, nobody will call you names. You are good and honest. All of us like you, no need to go anywhere; stay in my house and be happy.'

The Boss was lavishly flattering me. Mama looked at me with affection and sympathy. I noticed a smile blooming on her face.

My fury thawed away. As if it had rained in the desert wilderness.

I felt that my boss, like a camel in the desert, had stored up huge quantities of love inside of him, and was ready to share. It will all need fellow beings with a goodwill.

Venting the fury proves beneficial sometimes. As Madam was at an advanced stage of pregnancy, it was practically difficult to get another domestic worker on short notice. *That might be the reason for retaining me*, I thought.

Anyway, everything was for good.

I was at the zenith of happiness.

Thus, a new chapter of life was opening.

****

Chapter 13
A Friendly Boss

It was amazing, indeed. Certain situations can dramatically transform life. I had a salary hike, which could substantially cushion my financial difficulties.

Instead of calling me names, all of them called me Munthaya. I also was becoming an Arab, 'Karunakaran Al Munthaya.'

They were kind to me, orders were gentle. Welcome tranquility existed in the family, like the climate of the desert. The winter is abruptly ended with a dust storm and a drizzle, giving way to the summer. The same pattern is seen in my life also.

Big iron gates were opening up to me also. It was the calm after the storm. I was fortunate enough to work in a friendly environment for the first time. I was realizing that I too had a human identity and dignity.

'Ya Munthaya, please go to the supermarket; buy meat and chicken also.'

When days came to pass, I happened to be ubiquitous in all activities. Also, I had to supervise the family of the second wife of the Boss. They sought my opinion about the salary of the newly appointed maid, the home maintenance, and every other need. Thus, I became the confidante of the Boss and Madam. The Boss began to entrust me with the task of distributing the monthly pocket money to his children, 20 riyals each placed in white envelopes.

I became the supervisor of the newly employed people.

When the Madam delivered a baby, a driver from Bangladesh, Rahimul, also was appointed.

****

Chapter 14
To Alquire

Five years passed, and the entire family relocated to a new house built at Alquire, a village close to Darsait.

Alquire is a flatland, unlike Darsait, which was full of hills.

My Boss, in the meantime, got a promotion to the Ministry of Health. Outside of the new house, I was allotted a spacious room and a fairly big toilet for my own use.

The last time when I visited Kerala, Vasnathy had taken particular care to send a traditional butter lamp also in the baggage.

As the new dwelling offered me more privacy and space now, without fear or worry, I could light the traditional lamp and pray to Lord Krishna.

Twice or thrice, somehow, I had availed myself of opportunities to visit the temple downhill to pray to the Lord.

Kamal Musa of Baluchistan was one of the regular visitors to the house at Darsait. A few months after settling at Alquire, Kamal Musa married Madam's sister Rahat. She was a teacher at the school close to Alquire, and thus settled with Boss's family. Kamal Musa, a police officer of the Royal Police, became a member of the family.

Alquire had many Malayalees. It was a pleasure to celebrate my freedom with them. There was lush greenery all around, and I had hopes for the future. Even in the summer, I found cool vistas all around and a pleasant and tranquil working environment inside. I became more responsible, polite, and loyal in my duties.

Every Friday afternoon was a holiday to me. So, I could go to the junction close by and meet Malayalees. Thus, I could know what was happening all around. I developed deep solidarity with my compatriots.

My compatriot friends circle included Rafeeq, Shiyas, and Russel from Malappuram; Basheer from Kuttiadi; Salim from Trivandrum; and Abdul Khader from Palakkad.

****

Chapter 15
Driving Practice

Whenever new workers are needed, Boss and Madam would consult me. They consulted me before making any decision pertaining to the family and management. When a new driver was needed, it occurred to them that Munthaya could be trained to be one.

They engaged a trainer shortly; he was from Yemen. At home, I was familiar with the old Ambassador cars, operated by drivers by shifting the gear, by moving a lever attached under the steering wheel. At that time, I had taken no interest in knowing more about the machine.

My driving lessons were progressing. When I was competent enough to be on my own, I applied the accelerator, as usual, one day. The car was speeding. The teacher asked me to slow down, but I could not.

My foot was frozen, I was not able to move my foot.

'Are you going to kill yourself and take me along?' the teacher shouted. He was alarmed.

But I was helpless. The car was lurching ahead. There were huge palm trees bordering the road.

I also was frightened. I was not able to control the car. And I requested the trainer to intervene and stop the car somehow.

He managed to stop the car. The veins in my limbs were jutting out. The varicose vein problem, lying low over the years, came to the fore during the training.

'How can you become a driver in this state?' The driver was sympathetic and disappointed.

If necessary, given the clout of the Boss, I could procure a driving license. But I consulted a doctor, and I was advised to stay away from driving for some months and was asked to take a rest.

Madam threatened to deduct the three hundred riyals she had spent on me for driving practice, as I had failed her. But she did not actually do so. Yet she was very keen to see me as a qualified driver.

Whenever I was in financial cricis, I used to borrow from Madam two or three hundred riyals, it was deducted in installments from my salary. But when I had remitted hardly a hundred riyals, she would ask, 'How much did you pay back, Muntaya?'

'Ninety only, Madam,' I would say.

'Enough, the money due to me is waived. But next time I will recover the full amount, mark you.'

This cycle was repeated many times. She never took back the full amount of the loan. By pooling up the money, Madam asked me to keep, I could build a moderate house in my village.

****

Chapter 16
The Holy Lottery

I had cultivated strong connections with the Malayalee community. Uncle had brought many to the West Asian countries, capitalizing on his connections. Preman, one of my neighbors, reached our destination like that.

He was doing sundry, underpaid manual jobs to survive. One day he requested a salary hike. In the life of a slave, demanding a salary hike is blasphemous. The employer will not be amused by such demands. A salary hike, if at all, happens only when the employer has a whim to do so. The employer informed my uncle about the audacity.

'Has he grown so much? Let us pack him back home? Not a penny he deserves as a salary increment. He had the cheek to ask for a hike. We will cut him to size and show him the door,' the Uncle told the employer.

After a while, Preman was dismissed and sent back home.

After many months, when for the third time a phone call from a certain business establishment came to Madam, she gave me the phone. The manager of the firm conveyed an incredible message. Poor Preman had won the sales promotion lottery, a luxury premier Nissan car.

Preman had purchased four wristwatches from a shop at Ruwi, using the salary arrears he got upon leaving, after having served the company for four years. Along with the watches, he got a few coupons as part of the sales promotion during the month of Ramzan.

As I had been close to him, he had entered the phone number of my boss as the contact number on the coupon. The man who called informed me that the car could be claimed upon producing the coupon. I was happy for Preman, on whom fortune had smiled. But I wondered how to claim the same for the benefit of Preman.

I called him over the phone, and I was informed that the coupon was with his friends at Subee. I took a day off with the permission of the Boss, hailed a taxi to Subee, and recovered the coupon, claiming that the watches had to be repaired.

Then I went to the shop with the coupon, and the officer asked me about the owner of the coupon. I told him that Perman was out of the country. As per the punitive visa rules, he cannot return to the country for the next couple of years. The officer made a suggestion.

'I can arrange a bank draft worth Rs.400,000 (Rupees Four Hundred Thousand) for the car. It is a good price.'

'Sir, I must ask him; it is his coupon. I cannot take a decision myself. I will contact him; please give me a few days.'

When I came out, the Malayalee workers at the shop furtively informed me that the car was worth at least 700,000 rupees. They warned me not to sell it for Four Hundred Thousand Rupees. They were advising me out of goodwill. It was up to me to take a decision.

Preman had no phone connection at home. I had to call his neighbor, then call again after some time, allowing them time to summon Preman. I lost a fortune calling him time and again. But I wanted to make sure that the benefit reached the deserving hands. In the meantime, I tried another route, through one of my friends, to bring Preman on a tourist visa to this distant country. I spent 300 riyals to bring him to here. In his presence, I tried to bargain and sell the car.

As it was a distress sale, nobody suggested a reasonable price. Most of them did not have that kind of money. Raising a bank loan was a complicated process and out of bounds. So the maximum quoted price was 2000 riyals.

The market dynamics are such that demand, and price are correlated positively. The car had no demand. At last, in the presence of Preman, we sold the car to Kamal Moosa for 3800 riyals.

When he got the money, Preman became a different man. He was staying with me as a guest all those days, ever since he had arrived. He got furious with me on that day.

'You had offered to sell it for at least 500,000 Rupees. I trusted you. When I deduct the visa and travel expenses, I get almost nothing. You cheated on me. You played behind me to sell the car to that man. Probably you will get a commission for the deal.'

He was talking nonsense.

I was at a loss. I had spent my time and energy helping him. My friends had told me that Preman would give me at least 100,000 rupees for the pains I had taken for him, and I had said that I expected nothing; I wanted to help him, no strings attached. He had suffered here for a salary of 40 riyals. Now he has turned his guns on me.

I was devastated by the ingratitude of my friend, whom I had helped unconditionally.

Preman returned after a few days. But the scars he left behind on me remained.

****

Chapter 17
Thahira

Though I was enjoying more freedom and facilities, at night I was unable to sleep, and my mind was heavy. Sometimes I would get up in the still hours of the night and stay awake till morning.

My parents, Vasanthi, home, and village would gate crash into my mind. Like any other expatriate, running into millions, I used to struggle to get some sleep.

People are like that; we are greedy and look for more. We want to grab more and look around to get more.

But my ambition was to give more care and love to my mother and other members of the family. Even when I longed to spend quality time with my wife and mother when I reached home on leave, I spent time and money with my friends to realize the pleasures I had been denied in my childhood and I ignored the needs of my wife and mother.

Many thoughts haunted me. Ours was a small, thatched hut, with a suffocating, sooty kitchen in the corner, which had a heap of sooty, soiled earthen pots in the corner. My mother had to give birth to my brother in that space and I found her and the baby like a cat and kitten on the floor. I was asked to go and give one rupee to my mother, and when I reached home, I found her with the baby. When she tried to breastfeed my brother, as a twelve-year-old, I did not have the capacity or the wisdom to realize that my mother needed a little food in her stomach to feed him from her breast.

Thoughts were running wild.

It was past midnight; unable to sleep, I ventured out and surveyed the star-spangled heavens. Then I noticed a woman on the terrace of the nearby house, hanging washed clothes on the line to dry. I could see her close, as only a compound wall separated us. Immediately I recognized that she was a Malayalee.

'Are you a Malayalee? May I know your name?' I asked.

She was about fifty years old.

'Yes, baby, I am Thahira.'

'Why do you work at midnight? Sometimes I hear pots clashing in your kitchen at three in the morning. Are you alone in that house?'

'Baby, I am the only maidservant here. The Arab and his wife have ten children. I have to work day and night to meet the demand. I wash a hundred plates and vessels, then I have to do the laundry, which is followed by sweeping the compound. My back is breaking. Could you find another job for me? I want to escape.'

'Will you get a release from the sponsor?'

'I know nothing about it; if you can, please help me.'

Her misery touched me. Sleep had completely left me. I prayed to God to give me the power to help her.

Had I been at Darsait, I would have gone to the temple downhill to pray to the Lord to save Thahira.

I lit the traditional lamp and continued to pray for her. In my mind, pitiable images of Thahira flashed. I saw her washing the dirty linen and spreading it on the line. After reaching Alquire, Madam had given birth to her fifth child, Badr. The maid to look after the child was Lakshmi from Andhra Pradesh. Badr was a disabled child. The child could not speak properly. He conveyed his needs through gestures.

One day, as usual, Badr lifted his cup, indicating that he needed water. He was to be given warm water. But by mistake, Lakshmi served hot water from the kettle, which was meant for making tea. As Badr was incapable of telling hot and cold, he drank it all, scalding his mouth and alimentary canal.

I and Rahad rushed to him, hearing him cry in a peculiar way. This happened a week after my meeting with Thahira.

Lakshmi was summarily dismissed on that day and sent home. I was asked to find a replacement.

Availing of that opportunity, I mentioned Thahira case.

'She is hard working; I know her.'

Trusting me, Madam decided to appoint her and contacted her sponsor. Like an auction process, the haggling began. It was like the rich football clubs angling for players. At last, for 400 riyals, Thahira was released.

'Here you will be better off. Be good and dedicated, and you will be happy. The people here are very good. And I am here to support you,' I told her.

I expressed my gratitude to Lord Krishna for answering my prayer.

At that time, I was very pious. If you are earnest, God will answer you, folks. Experience has taught me that. I had prayed so much for Thahira, whom I hardly knew, and I prayed for her with tears from the bottom of my heart.

****

Chapter 18
In and Out

Domestic workers, including drivers, leaving and joining new ones are common in my boss's house. While leaving their job, some accused Madam of having ill-treated them or had behaved rudely to them. The servants will not stay for long. Her tempestuous nature used to scare away the servants.

During my tenure there, four drivers were hired and fired. They were pressurized to accomplish the mission assigned to them in no time. When they were asked to bring food from a hotel, Madam expected them to bring it instantly. But the hotel people would take time to pack and serve the food. Still, she refused to acknowledge the ground reality and blasted them. The drivers often told me their predicament.

When the latest driver was dismissed, it was my duty to find another one.

'Munthaya, find another driver immediately,' she ordered.

When Madam makes a demand, I cannot fail her or let her down. I traced out one Mr. Jayan from Thrissur, who was a pick up-van driver on a date palm farm. I spirited him away and offered 30 riyals as an additional salary.

Jayan was not an expert driver. He was not used to busy roads and urban areas. And he was not familiar with the territory and road network. He had poor navigational skills and used to lose his way very often.

Alquire had many squares, and he used to mark directions at each square by placing wood splinters there, indicating the direction to take.

He did not care for traffic rules. Madam also noticed his crude driving. Still, he held his head high.

Every driver is supposed to wash and clean the car he is in charge of. But Jayan refused to do it and used to shout at me when food was not served on time. Also, he was taken to backbiting and vicious gossip. Actually, I offered this job to him, understanding that he was languishing on the farm with a paltry salary. But he was forgetting his past, just like forgetting the routes while driving.

'I want a leave of absence today; I want to meet with a friend,' Jayan asked on the very first Friday when he had hardly completed four days on his new job.'

I was stunned by his demand, and I explained to him gently.

'Cool down, Jayan; you have hardly completed four days here. How can you demand an off day so early? Today, being a Friday, we have a busy day. We can have our way slowly. Today, you have to go with us. I am doing all the work here, and they never gave me a weekly half day off till recently. I don't get leave sanctioned when asked. And I ask only when it is extremely important. In the afternoon, I could take you with me, tactfully getting their permission. Now you please cool down.'

'I cannot be an underdog like you. I took the job because you offered a weekly leave, and now you are breaking the contract.'

'Jayan, leave is sanctioned by Madam. You cannot take leave without her permission. You are new here; who is your friend here?'

'It is none of your business; I need a leave today; you are responsible for that.'

Jayan was recalcitrant. He was nagging me. Then I contacted Khais, the son-in-law of the Boss and Jayan's sponsor, and told him the situation.

He immediately contacted Madam and asked to sanction a leave of absence. I thought that it was the normal procedure. He was the official sponsor of Jayan. He should know what was happening.

Madam blew her top when Khais requested so. She yelled with fire and fury in her eyes.

'In what capacity you contacted Khais above my head on behalf of the driver? Why the hell did you do it? Jayan is my employee, and I am the authority. Are you playing tricks with me? Have you grown too big for me, Munthaya? Get out from my house; you are done; get out of my house this moment.'

I was stunned. I had been supervising everything in the family, and everybody respected me. Suddenly I was served the ultimatum. How can that lady degrade so? I was speechless. The Boss was not home, and the house plunged into disarray. Even the Boss was never able to tame her, hers was the last word in the family often, being a school principal.

Jayan, realizing that the situation is bad, made himself scarce, hiding in his room.

The children wept, looking at me. They pleaded with tears, 'Don't go, Munthaya, don't go.'

Mama, Rehab, and everybody else in the house affectionately advised her and reasoned with her.

'No matter what, it is not fair to dismiss Munthaya.'

Madam was dead to all entreaties as rage and congenital ego got the better of her.

'He slighted me; he has no place in my house. I will not entertain any appeals on that.' Madam was obstinate.

Rehab and Mama warned her that she alone will be responsible for all the consequences when Munthaya is gone. Still, she was resolute.

I dreaded that that murderously hysterical woman may take her own life in the fury.

I stuffed my things in a bag and went into hiding in the latrine outside.

Madam came to my room, made sure that I was gone, and locked up the room.

I had lost everything in an emotional tsunami. I wanted to inform my boss, who was at the second wife's place, but I did not have the strength after the ambush by Madam.

I sneaked out and went to my friend's shop at the junction and sat there. I would be in deep crisis if I lost that job.

Back at home, what job would I be fit for? I had already reached the threshold of middle age. The quarry job teasingly beckoned. I peeped down into the formidable quarry pit.

I telephoned Kamal Moosa for a solution.

'No problem; you stay there; I am coming to you. We will fix it; stay cool.' Kamal consoled me and came to where I was with his car.

I went back, hiding in his car, and dove into the darkness of the latrine.

After some time, Kamal and the Boss came out and knocked on the door.

'Munthaya, you know her nature. Go and ask her forgiveness. It will solve everything. She will forgive, we both will be with you; let us go.'

'Boss, I did not commit anything wrong. Why should I seek forgiveness? What did I do to seek forgiveness? I serve you, but I too have fundamental self-esteem.'

I talked as if I had quarreled with my mother or wife. I was on the verge of tears as I felt humiliated for nothing.

'Munthaya, if a word "sorry" would solve everything, just say it. You could continue the job with dignity, or do you want to go back home?'

I could not defy my boss. More than that, the job was a matter of life and death to me. Madam was sitting on the sofa in a belligerent mood to pounce on any victim. That possessed woman needed prey to vent her spleen, and I happened to be the first in line. I went to her with a pounding heart.

My consolation was that the Boss was with me. I went to her, confessed my mistake, and sought her forgiveness.

'Madam, if I did anything presumptuous on the driver's leave issue, I seek your forgiveness.'

The red-hot lady was on the verge of an explosion. But my words instantly quenched her fury. The ego and rage of some people are very short-lived.

'Hm, if you repeat it, I will finish you. This time you are forgiven.'

She flung the key to my room in my direction. When I picked it up from the floor, once again I became the Karuanakaran, who picked up cooked rice balls on the floor, thrown into the leaf of the poor workers by the Namboothiri's men.

But if I had not been taken back, I would not have been here the way I am.

****

Chapter 19
The Fruit Boxes

Mariam, Mama's sister, passed away. In Arab culture, if a relative is dead, they go to the family of the bereaved after a few days with fruits and delicacies. They would also distribute fruits to all.

Mama asked me to go to the market and buy fruits.

'I want to take it to my sister's place, and I have to distribute fruits to people all around.'

Mama gave me 400 riyals, and Madam, standing close, suggested, 'Muntaya, don't go alone; take Jamal also.'

Mama objected to it, 'No need to take Jamal along; let him go with the driver.'

I went to the fruit and vegetable market and bought different kinds of fruit in large quantities and loaded the van. The total cost was only 175 riyals.

We stacked up the fruit boxes in the large kitchen room, and they occupied half of the space. Then I went to Mama to return the balance amount.

Mama got annoyed. 'Muntaya, I had asked you to buy fruits for 400 riyals, and you bought a little bit only. I cannot go to my relatives like that. Go to the market again and buy fruits for the rest of the amount as well.'

'Mama, please come with me; let me show you. If it is not enough, I will go again.'

Mama and Madam came to the kitchen to inspect, and they were astonished by the volume of the stacks.

'Are you bluffing? Did you really get this for just 175 riyals? What happened? Did you buy damaged and third-rate fruits from the market?' Madam asked.

'It is of the best quality, Madam. Do not be skeptical. If you want, we could open and examine each box right away. I spent only 175 riyals for the entire cargo.'

Just like a mother who prides herself on the honesty of her son, Mama pointed me to Madam and told her, 'Look how efficiently Munthaya manages things. He could have taken the whole amount, and we would never suspect him. If Jamal was there, he would have claimed to have spent the whole amount and would have asked for more money. Munthaya is honest and good. Do return 50 riyals to him form the balance amount.'

Madam, quite pleased, gave me 50 riyals.

****

Chapter 20
I Miss Home

The wheel of time rolled on, repeating the cycle of autumn, winter, spring, and summer. Time takes no holiday, and people get old.

'Are you conscious of the fact that we have two daughters?' Vasanthy used to remind me.

In fact, I was not very serious about that fact.

My tongue was used to the words sir, madam, and mama; I had little need for other words. Back at home, I squandered my holidays with friends and visiting relations and flew back to the Gulf state.

'Do put a stop to this kind of life. Now we have a small house of our own. God will help us to marry away our daughters.' Each time Vasanthy would fall at my feet begging to stay back.

The women at home usually tell this to the expatriate husbands.

Did I care for Vasanthy sufficiently? While in the village, I used to hit home late at night, freaking out with my friends, and enjoying my financial freedom, which was denied to me during my youthful years.

On a sleepless night, I remembered that a hornet's nest was disturbed in my mind.

Before going to bed, you should rescind all foreboding thoughts. With a light mind, you should go to sleep. I know this psychological reality, but still, heavy thoughts continued to haunt me.

Now, my father is no more, my mother must be lonely. Though I have four people to stick to, I am actually alone here. Vasanthy also must be lonely; she was denied by her husband.

The frequency of phone calls to home inadvertently increased, and so did the duration too.

I would regularly ask Vasanthy, 'And what else?' and lately Vasanthy has been very cold in her response.

Long back, she would wait for my phone calls. Now she seldom picks up the phone. When I get up in the morning, if I find a missed call from her end, I can rest assured that she is safe. But lately, it is more difficult to get her or the children on the phone.

Vasanthy was changing; she was not energetic anymore, and sometimes she spoke to me as if to a stranger. She would say absurd things. I realized that she needed psychological treatment.

I struggled to sleep. The next day, I could not concentrate on my duties. I took more time to wash the car. Usually, I would splash water on the car with a hose and rub the surface clean using cotton. But I lost my rhythm.

I tried to recollect the fifteen years I had spent as a servile and humble servant. It was a life saturated with ups and downs, sweetness and bitterness.

My blood pressure was climbing up contemplating my people at home. Do my people think of me the way I do? I had heard of telepathy; was it affecting me? My mother will think of me, for sure. I had a splitting headache. I sat on the bed, supporting my chin with my hands. Had Vasanthy been with me! Had I been able to lay my head on my mother's lap!

'Father, let me apply balm on your forehead,' my daughter was soothing me. I slipped into slumber.

****

Chapter 21
The Castles in the Air

Each time my thought upon returning from home was to make some money and go back at the earliest.

The next time when I go back, I want to take Vasanthy and the children on a merry trip. It may make her happy. And she needs the support of a psychiatrist to recover.

My thoughts were flying home.

On a day of drizzling, I went to the post office at Alquire, around 10 a.m. in Morning. The postal goods are sorted and placed in different chests meant for specific addressees. I entered the large hall and headed to the chest meant for my boss. On the smooth floor, my feet hit something solid.

It was a small black-colored purse. I picked it up, and it had 450 riyals. Then I found some phone numbers and the name of the owner in different pouches. It belonged to one K. M. Rajesh, obviously a Malayalee.

When I came out with the postal goods, I noticed a young man sadly searching on the ground. He came to me and asked, 'Brother, did you by any chance see a purse here on the floor? I had been here just ten minutes ago. When I searched for my purse to send money home at the money exchange, I found it missing. I did not go anywhere else. Could you help me? My sister's wedding is fixed for the next week. This money I had saved for that.'

The young man was on the verge of tears.

My mad thoughts of going home with the booty were suddenly grounded. I imagined his parents and his sister, ready to get married, sitting detected. I chased away the devil inside me, and the good prevailed over the evil. I asked him many personal questions to check the veracity of his claims. When I realized that the purse was his, I returned it with pleasure. And the happiness registered in his eyes was ineffable. The construction worker embraced me.

'God brought you here, brother. If it had fallen into the hands of an evil man, I would have been shedding my tears helplessly.'

'Brother, please accept this, not as a reward, it is for my satisfaction. God will reward you. God will be merciful to you; do accept this.'

He offered me 10 riyals.

I dismissed the youth from Kollam, stating that I did not deserve it and that I had only done what was humane.

****

Chapter 22
The Wheel of Time

Many more years came to pass.

I visited my family on a yearly basis, and it had become a routine. Each time I went home, I did so with a resolution not to return, and upon returning, I would long for stopping it all and hitting home. But after every vacation, like a ball kicked to the wall or like a piece of iron attracted to a magnet, I went back to my boss.

On each visit home, just to see the happiness, contentment, and hope, I showered them with exotic gadgets they were not familiar with. I silently reveled in the appeal and good name our family was getting in society because of money.

Each time I returned from home, my energy was draining. Age was telling on me. My dreams seemed to be less colorful, and many of my dreams had faded.

I was at the threshold of middle age, and I had slept most part of my life on a single bed, did the same jobs, faced the same people, and listening to the same sounds. But everybody was aging. An old house could be repaired and repainted to look young. What could be done to make life young again? Could I do something new in that house? Could we seek new pastures of excitement?

My life was under the control of the prevailing laws of an alien land and the whims, likes, and dislikes of the Boss and his imperious wife. I was subject to the likes and dislikes of Madam and the Boss and the peculiar domestic environment they had created. Expatriate life is a modern prison life, and an annual visit home is brief parole. The voluntary prison life lasts until the expatriate chooses to go back home forever. In this prison life, the defendant, lawyer, judge, and all are a single person. His crime is that he wanted to give a better life to his dear and near ones. For some people, expatriate life is in effect a hejira from the unpalatable realities of life.

'I am living here happily, minding my own business. I could give a damn what happens to others.'

I would often reason so, but I failed to be that thick. My family was weighing on me, but I had not saved for a rainy day. I had shared everything I had, and nothing was left for me. There was no financial security to face an uncertain tomorrow.

I was considerate to all; I cared for my family, siblings, relations, and friends.

One day Thahira told me, observing my swollen cheeks and wrinkled face, which had the shadow of a lost youthfulness, 'Karunakara, you are getting old.'

'Yes, sister, the time has taken it all, health and charm. I have to reconcile with the ground realities. Look at our boss; I have been serving him for more than twenty-five years. Long back, he had an imposing and commanding personality. Now he is in a high position in business and job. But age has caught up with him. He is not brisk and does not have that commanding power. Time is not merciful to anybody.'

I observed my face in the mirror. The pepper and salt hair, the grey beard, and the weak face told me where I was headed. If I did not shave in the morning, white stubble used to stick out to proclaim my age.

The situation at home perturbed me. My BP problem was not under control, in spite of the tablets. The ultimate panacea is a passage to my home country once and for all. After twenty-seven years, a return was inevitable. With all the savings, I had built a house and two partially completed shop rooms too. It had to be completed. What shall I do at home? How shall we live? Nobody knows.

My single mission was to go back home. The Boss, Madam, Mama, and other people in the family, and the friends at the junction are all strangers to me. They are not part of my life in the final reckoning.

****

Chapter 23
Boss – the Patriarch

I prefer to consider my boss as my elder brother, now that he is in his seventies. Nay, I treat him as my own elder brother. Boss was my personal pride. He was closer to me than my own uncle, Sreedharan. In the dear words of human speech, I cannot express my love for him.

I wonder what force made us so close and intimate, even though he had spurned me and treated me like dirt or a mean slave. What was the chemistry? Now he needs me in everything, he depended on me.

On that night, my thoughts were running wild.

The next morning, I went to the Boss when he was about to drive away in his car. I said softly, 'Boss, I want to go home.'

He looked into my face nonchalantly.

'What is the urgency? How long have you been here after the last visit home?'

'Ten months, boss. I am not asking for a leave of absence.'

'Then?'

'I want to go back home forever.'

I said so, diverting my eyes to the plants in full bloom. The Boss did not say anything. He drove away as if nothing had happened.

I wonder how I managed to tell him my decision. I was trembling from top to toe. I had not given much thought as to how Boss would react to the bombshell of a request.

'Why did you tell me yesterday that you wanted to leave?' he asked me the next day.

Then I told him that I wanted to relocate permanently to my home village, and he was suddenly gloomy.

'Did you think well? What is your problem back at home? You had told me that you had another daughter to be married away and that you were pooling up money for her dowry. Then why do you suddenly change your mind on short notice?'

Boss asked me after waking up from his long reverie.

'At home, my mother, wife, and daughter are not safe. They have nobody but me, sir. My wife is having psychological issues because of my absence. Now I have to be with her. I must go.' My reaction was solid and premeditated.

Immediately, the Boss conveyed the message to Madam. She was shocked.

'Munthaya, if you go, we will be in a fix. If you are telling the truth, if you are determined, we will make arrangements for your journey back home next week. We will take return tickets too for you so that you could come back in a month or two if you change your mind. But think well and go home to come back.'

The Boss told me before going to bed.

It was difficult to kill time for a week. Using the money, I had, I purchased many things for the family, as I used to do every time before going home. I revealed my decision to my friends at the junction. They were taken aback.

After a couple of days, they organized a send-off meeting at their place. Rafeeq, Nishad, Russell, Saleem, and Abdulkhader, my dear friends, hugged me and buttressed their friendship with me.

They seemed to tell me that humanism is the basis of friendship and that a humane approach should be the underlying principle of any ideology.

When the Babri Masjid was demolished, some Muslim employees under the Boss from Bangalore confided in him, 'Hindus demolished the holy mosque. Hence, it is time to give a fitting lesson to all Hindus here. They are not trustworthy; better dismiss them.'

'As a Muslim, I am saddened that the mosque was destroyed by the vandals. But those who did it have no values, have no religion. That is why they committed such a diabolic atrocity. Still, all Indians are not like them. As an employer, I am concerned only about performance, honesty, and deliverability. You must be reliable and should have basic integrity. I do not care about other things. If my employees do something against the grain of these policies, I will take appropriate action, irrespective of religion. Munthaya is the most dedicated employee at home. I entrust everything to him. He is part of my family. I never asked what religion he was. He never mentioned it either. I have reprimanded him when he made mistakes.' My boss shut the gossiping mouths. I came out to know about this from Jayan.

When my friends hugged me and smothered me with overwhelming love, I remembered the stance taken by the Boss. I was full of tears when they loved me so much.

That night, I walked home from the room.

****

Chapter 24
Back to the Roots

July at Alquire is just like the blazing sun.

My mind also was simmering. Twenty-seven years ago, I landed up in this country in another blazing July. Unlike other people, I never sought another sponsor; I served the same master and did the same job. Many people tried their luck with different sponsors, and some were successful and some were not. Now, Karunakaran, the judge, has passed the verdict to free himself from the jail that he had assiduously built around him.

Sleep evaded me.

'Munthaya, how is this maidservant? What do you think? would she become a good domestic maid servant at home?'

Madam would ask me while visiting the agency that offers maidservants.

My boss would ask at the car showroom, 'What do you think about this car? Did you like the model? Is it good?'

Munthaya had begun as a servile slave, then a worker, and now he is the supervisor. Madam and boss would seek my opinion on any familial or personal matters. The children would first approach Munthaya to get things done through the parents. My word carried water in all matters.

Often, mind becomes an infinite ocean; thoughts are the waves that crash against the distant shores and return to the ocean. What is so particular about me? I am just yet another ordinary mortal. Why do I magnify myself? Many millions had migrated to the oil-rich Arab Gulf to eke out a living, and I was only one among them.

I could stay back if needed. Then why should I be carried away by the passions? I had been staying awake and thinking from three in the morning. Thoughts have no end of the road.

At least by 9:30 a.m., I decided, I must go to the airport with the driver. My boss had handed over to me the passport and travel documents on the previous night, and a high tide of thoughts heaved up.

I thought I was choking; there was no movement down the esophagus. And a volcano was on the verge of eruption in my head.

When I got up, it was already 10 am. I was not hungry; I did not even need a cup of tea. I took bath and changed. I got ready to say goodbye to the people in the house. I needed strength to face the situation. I prayed to God to have the strength to handle the high-voltage moments.

My feet were heavy.

An emergency conclave was on in the hall. My boss was presiding over. The agenda was Munthaya's departure. They seemed to have understood the fact that the roots of an individual cannot be severed. Munthaya had been a rootless, floating being in that family all these years.

'Here is my contribution, 500 riyal; here is mine, 300; take this 400 riyals; here is my 200 Riyals.'

All the earning members of the family, men and women, were contributing money into the hands of my boss.

I met each one. I was sorry for the imbecile child Badr and the undergrowth child Abeer. I prayed for the children.

At last, I had to go to Mama. I was on the verge of tears upon seeing Mama struggling to contain her grief. Mama was my mother for more than 27 years. She was my mother and support. Perhaps I had given her more care and love than my biological mother.

I went to her and collected her frail hands into mine.

'Your son is waiting for me, Mama. I must be going. It is time to go. You are a mother to me, though you did not give birth to me. Forgive me and bless me.'

'Munthaya, ya Munthaya.' Her ancient eyes spilled over; she held my hands.

'Stay back, Munthaya; you will have no problem here. Stay back.'

Her grip was getting stronger with each word uttered. I could not contain my tears. I had no words to console her. I freed myself from her wattle-thin hands and walked away, choking for words.

'Munthaya, God will bless you,' she raised her hand and whispered.

'Munthaya, let us know if you ever have any need.' Noora and Afra shed tears.

Badr, with whom I used to walk outside the compound, smiled at me innocently. Abeer, realizing that I was going somewhere, waved her white hand as a way of saying goodbye.

'Your luggage is in my car; I and Mohamed will take you to the airport.'

Hearing that, I burst into tears with happiness. My boss was surprising me with his gestures of kindness and care.

Over the years, I had worked with thirty different domestic servants, men and women. Now, at the time of my departure, there were Mallika from Sri Lanka, Nisa from the Philippines, and Thahira.

All of them were apprehensive, as if something sinister was going to happen to them. Unable to suffer through the emotional moments, I was getting weak. I was crying and collapsing inside. I touched the feet of my boss as if we might not meet again.

The huge iron gate that I used to close every day was opened to me for the last time. The luxury Mercedes S-class car of the boss floated down the road to Muscat international airport.

I went to my boss, as we were not likely to meet again.

'Boss, we may not meet again. All the 27 years, I have been loyal to you. I seek forgiveness for any lapses from my side. In my country, government servants are considered lucky. They get a monthly pension after retirement. It is more than enough to help them live a dignified life. I spent my youthful years here with you. I have no idea how to survive back at home in my declining years. Even if I don't have a monthly pension, we will survive, and we will be contented and happy as a family. Thus, my life will come to a peaceful end. Let me go back home, sir.'

The security check was really fast, and I procured the boarding pass to wait in the waiting room. When I looked out, my master and his son Mohamed were still standing there, and my master's eyes were spilling out. He pulled out his shawl from his shoulder and wiped his tears. Then he got into his car and drove away.

The huge air plane died into the blue infinity of the heavens, heading toward Calicut International Airport, carrying me.

****

Chapter 25
Relocated

I was back home, forever.

After the warm reception at home, I was on the move for a week. I was taking the gifts given to me for delivery at various houses as requested by my friends at the junction at Alquire. Also, some friends had specifically asked me to visit their houses without fail. Thus, a few days passed by. Still, the nagging thought on my mind was how to make a living in the new circumstances.

My bank balance was almost nil. But I thought of opening a grocery shop in the rooms designed as a commercial building. The cash gifted to me by the boss and his family amounted to 400,000 rupees.

Like many other expatriates, having no experience in business, I also invested the entire amount at the grocery. Some of my concerned relatives warned me against it, but the people of my village wholeheartedly supported the move.

The two rooms were full of commercial goods, and I could not vigilantly watch over the things. Vasanthy, who used to fall at my feet, asking me to stay back, was altogether frigid and cold to me. Still, she also came to the shop to support me when she was free.

Even today, I regret that I went all the way out to satisfy my friends, relatives, and siblings by ignoring my own family. I had saved nothing for my family.

When Vasanthy's family property share was registered, the twenty cents of land, which was not at a prime location, I insisted that it may be registered collectively in my and my wife's name. Her parents did not object to it, as I had the image of a gentleman. Though I am not a go-getter, an invisible force asked me to demand it, and Vasanthy's people agreed to it. Though I have no land of my own, through her I got a small tract of land under joint ownership.

I had finished six weeks in my village, and I got a phone call from Western Union Money Exchange. I was requested to visit its office at Thaliaparamba to collect ten thousand rupees. I engaged Vasanthy in the shop and went to Thalipparamba. To my surprise, my master, Salem Abdulla, had sent the money.

After receiving the money, I called the boss over the phone and asked him why he had done so.

'Munthaya, you need money to live comfortably. I am worried about your well-being. You had mentioned that government servants are privileged to get a monthly pension. This is the pension for the services you rendered and this should be secret between us; let nobody know it.'

'I will pray to God for you and your family, sir.'

Even when I hung up, I was wonderstruck. I wanted to share this moment of happiness with Vasanthy. Once Kamal Moosa told me over the phone that my boss had lamented to him that his right hand, Munthaya, was eternally gone from him.

Months passed by. One day, a friend of mine employed in the Near Eastern region, came to visit me, and, inter alia, I mentioned my boss and his largesse in the form of a monthly pension. My friend was surprised by the marvelous and humane Arab; it was helping me cushion my impending financial difficulties at home and in the continuing education of my daughter. He insisted on getting introduced to the Arab, who was the personification of goodness. I telephoned the boss and gave the phone to my friend, who was anxious to talk. He extolled and praised my boss.

After the dialogue, my boss was annoyed with me.

'I had told you that this must be a secret.'

The shop was launched, purportedly, by the filthy rich Gulf returnee, to dissipate his wealth. Things were going bad. When I entertained customers in one room, in the other they were busy stealing away the goods. I was unable to be present in both rooms. At last, the creditors who refused to clear the bills and the thieves together put the enterprise in sick bed.

The monthly pension offered by the boss helped me survive, buffering the crisis. The money invested in the shop was lost to creditors and thieves, and I called my boss to tell him about the situation at home. My boss chastised me for being a naivete and asked me not to be a simpleton. He gave me another 200,000 rupees to begin it all over again. My master never ceased to surprise me with his gestures of care, love, mercy, and largesse.

In addition to the monthly pension, once I got another 20, 000 rupees, Mama used to talk to me over video calls on the smartphone used by Mallika.

'He is like my son, which is why I had a dream about him and I have send the money today itself,' the next morning, she told Mallika.

On a Ramzan, Afra, the daughter of my master, sent Rs. 5,000 to me. She used to send different amounts on and off. The children did not forget their Munthaya, who handheld them across the difficult terrains of life.

Thahira's daughter called me from Ernakulam.

'Mother is very sick. She has a tumor in her brain. Immediate surgery is needed. She wants to see you before the surgery. Will you come?'

Thahira had been in her house for many months. She had come to India a couple of years back. She used to remember me with affection and gratitude for offering her a job in the house of my boss. She used to bring gifts for me whenever she came on vacation. Also, she used to bring me things I would ask her to bring from abroad. Thahira was the only earning member of the family. Her husband was not caring for the family, which I had realized long ago. I was sure that she had financial difficulties to meet the surgery expenses.

I informed my boss about the development. He quizzed me for some time to get a real picture. Later, he sent Rs. 200,000 to my account to meet her surgery expenses. But the surgery funded by my boss failed to serve the purpose. After a few months, Thahira was called to meet her maker in heaven.

Twelve years had passed since I settled in my village. Long back, my relatives and friends used to compete enviously to invite me to their houses and offer me a treat.

I had struggled a great deal to reach everywhere and please everybody. After settling here, all of my friends and relatives seemed to have forgotten me.

At Alquire, in the house of my master, I had only a single cot as my own. Here in my village, the same is the case. Though the house is jointly owned by me and my wife.

Most of the expatriates end up in a state of an abandoned mine or an invalidated currency note.

The employees at the Bank of Baroda branch are surprised about the 10,000 rupees changed hands every month. The boss and his erstwhile supervisor, Karunakaran Nambiar, are their cherished customers now.

'Friends, see for yourself the mercy and care of my great master on me. This month's pension has already been credited to my account.'

He raised his mobile phone and brandished the SMS from the Bank of Baroda.

****